# *My Dear Muslim Brother Don't Show off*

Yasir Nouman Suleiman

In the Name of Allah, The Most Merciful, The
Bestower of Mercy.

Praise be to Allah, peace and blessings be upon our Prophet Muhammad, as well as his family and all his companions.

Education and purification of the soul is a very important matter. Despite this, some people show great carelessness in relation to education. There are many opportunities in our lives to do good, and many are willing to follow this path, do good and encourage others to do the same. However, often a person who wants to act correctly makes a mistake, he wants to follow a straight and clear road, but he is mistaken and comes to a dead end. One of the reasons for this is inattention to work on the correction of one's soul. As soon as a man aspires to some good cause, Satan tries to deceive him, his weak heart becomes a good riding vehicle for the vile tempter, on which the Satan is very comfortable to sit and manage. He uses his favorite reins to control the soul: show-off, the desire for fame, greatness and praise, narcissism, the desire for superiority over others. With these reins, Satan entangles his inexperienced victim so that he or she has as few opportunities as possible to rebel against him.

In order to avoid this, it is necessary to hold fast to sincerity (ikhlas), which is the true essence of the Islamic Religion and the key of the Prophetic call.

Allah Almighty said:

"But they were ordered only to worship Allah, serving him sincerely."
(Quran 98:4)

"Blessed is He in Whose Hand is dominion, Who is capable of all things, Who created death and life, to test you and see whose deeds are better."
(Quran 67:12)

Fudayl ibn Iyad, commenting on this verse, said that the best deeds are the most sincere and most correct deeds from the point of view of Shariah.

In one of the great hadiths, which is the foundation of the foundations of Islam, the Messenger of Allah (peace and blessings of Allah be upon him) said:

"Deeds are evaluated in accordance with intentions, and each person will receive only what he intended to receive" (hadith narrated by al-Bukhari and Muslim).

The Prophet (peace and blessings of Allah be upon him) also said:

"The harm from two starving wolves directed to sheep is no more for them than the harm for a person from the desire to achieve wealth and respect at the expense of their religion" (hadith was cited by at-Tirmidhi).

Ibn Taymiyyah (may Allah grant him mercy) said: "Sincerity is the most important of the deeds of the heart, which in turn is a component of such a thing as Faith. This is the greatest and most honorable deed." The work of the heart in general is much more significant and important than the actions performed by the body. Therefore, let a Muslim not be deceived and remember that obedience to the commands of Allah without sincerity and truthfulness in relations with Him has no value and there will be no reward for it. Moreover, a person deprived of sincerity in his actions is in great danger, even if his good deeds are related to such great deeds as spending property for good purposes and fighting for the Faith.

And even religious knowledge, through which Allah grants many benefits to peoples and countries, can be a danger to their bearer if he does not honestly and sincerely practice his Religion for the sake of Allah (the Great and Glorious). The Messenger of Allah (peace and blessings of Allah be upon him) said:

"Whoever has learned the knowledge through which one should strive for the Face of Allah (He is Great and Glorious), only in order to receive something from the blessings of this world, he will not even feel the smell of Paradise on the Day of Judgment" (hadith narrated by Abu Dawud).

With the permission of Allah, we will consider several properties of the soul that can destroy their owner.

1) Love for praise. A person who loves praise experiences great joy and exultation when they speak well of him in the presence of people and praise him.

Al-Hasan ibn Ziyad said: "Shaitan will not leave a person until he applies all possible tricks to him, he tries to extract something from a person that will let other people know about his deeds. For example, if a person makes many circuits around the Kaaba (tawaf), then [the devil encourages him to say in front of others]: "How beautiful was the circuit around the Kaaba this night!" Or a person fasts, and [the devil encourages him to say]: "How hard it is to eat in the morning [before fasting] (suhoor)" or "How much I want to drink." Try, if possible, not to talk, say, or read in public. If you are eloquent, then people will say: "How well he speaks, how beautiful his speech is, what a wonderful voice." Then you will like their words, and you will become proud. If you do not show eloquence, then people will say: "He does not know how to speak, and his voice is ugly." Then their words will upset you, and you will fall into a show. If you can speak without worrying about people's praise or blame, then speak.

2) Frequent mention of their affairs. This includes the conversations of a person about how much he has undergone difficulties, how much he had to endure, what trials fell to his lot. It is possible that outwardly this may look like an expression of love for this Religion and is done to awaken enthusiasm and stamina in other Muslims, but in fact, deep down it is only a desire to show one's personal virtues and demonstrate one's stamina in the spread of the Religion. Often a person does this in order to earn the respect of people, win their hearts and win their praise.

Al-Qurtubi (may Allah grant him mercy) said: "The essence of showing off is the desire to achieve the benefits of this world through deeds of worship, and at its core this desire to achieve honor in the hearts of people."

3) Attributing to oneself the deeds done by several people. This is expressed in the fact that a person likes to show superiors and ordinary people that he is the central person in some business or project, that it was he who did all the main work, that he invented everything so well, that he advised, etc. Such claims, as they grow, can lead to even greater danger, and a person will begin to ascribe to himself what he did not do at all. Allah Almighty said about such people:

"Do not think that those who rejoice in their deeds and love to be praised for what they have not done will be saved from torment. They are destined for painful suffering." (Quran 3:188)

4) Inflated modesty. Some people show modesty and lack of pride in order to get a positive assessment from people so that they praise his worthy behavior. People will say: "What a well-mannered man, how reserved, how tactful." But in fact, he is dead.

5) Mention of numerous visitors and guests. This is expressed in the fact that a person mentions the multitude of those who come to him. He can talk about it, expressing his dissatisfaction that these visitors do not leave him time to read books and gain knowledge. Actually, this is a trick of Satan. Such a person seems to be waiting to be asked about how he obtains knowledge or does some kind of work, in order to answer to inform the interlocutor about his extreme busyness with people's problems, that they often come to him because they have a great need for him, and it takes him a long time.

Saad ibn Abdullah said: Great and insightful scholars pondered over the interpretation of sincerity, and found nothing but the following interpretation: "Any movement and any immobility of a person, everything secret and obvious should be only for the sake of Allah, nothing should be mixed with this intention, neither one's own ego, nor personal desires, nor the goods of this world."

6) Self-admiration. A person whose soul is afflicted with the disease of narcissism happily says about himself: "I showed diligence and selflessness, helping people, I did this and that ... Yesterday I did not close my eyes, thinking and worrying about the situation of Muslims," etc. At the same time, a person does not suspect that he has already fallen into one of the devil's networks.

Masruk said: "If a person fears Allah, then he has enough knowledge. If a person admires his deeds, then he has enough ignorance.

Defining "narcissism", Abdullah ibn al-Mubarak said:

"This is a demonstration in front of people of what you have, but others do not."

Ibn al-Qayyim said: "There is nothing more harmful for good deeds than narcissism and self-admiration, and there is nothing more useful for good deeds than understanding and recognizing the mercy of Allah and His assistance, as well as relying on His help, a feeling of constant need for Him and sincerity in deeds dedication to Him."

Remember the person whom the Messenger of Allah (peace and blessings of Allah be upon him) told us about in one of his hadiths. He said:

"One man walked importantly in his jewelry, he admired himself, then Allah ordered the earth to seize him, and he plunged into it with a roar until the Day of Judgment" (hadith narrated by al-Bukhari and Muslim).

7) Using every opportunity to announce their affairs. This is expressed in the fact that a person is looking for an opportunity to show off his knowledge. and mention your blessings. If in a conversation someone utters, for example, the word "Asia", then this person will immediately remember that he is an expert on Asia, knows everything and everything there. If someone says the word "Africa", then this person will need to mention that he spent ten years there in search of knowledge. If the conversation goes about some city, then he will definitely note that he has traveled there more than once for the purpose of enlistment and for lectures. If they are talking about a village, then it will be impossible not to say that he went there with his brothers to bring help to needy Muslims. If someone starts talking about some successful charitable project, then it will immediately become known to everyone firsthand that this person stood at the origins of this project, encouraged people, and only after a long, hard and persistent work on his part did they agree, and only then did it work. If during the conversation the topic of the poor is touched upon, then this person will reveal to you his extraordinary outlook regarding the situation of the needy, because he has been dealing with this problem for a long time and takes care of

the poor. If the conversation is about the call to Islam and the guidance of the lost, then this person will list you all who accepted Islam from his call and remember how many people stood on righteous path, thanks to him.

This person forgets that he should do righteous deeds not in order to later publicly declare them, and not to please someone's ears or increase his own self-esteem. All righteous deeds are a road supply on a long journey to their Lord, and this supply is rapidly consumed if a person turns off the path and rushes to the satisfaction of people. A person often forgets that good deeds are, first of all, the mercy of Allah to him, and not vice versa. The one who does good should not expect gratitude from people, but on the contrary, he himself is obliged to thank Allah for the gifts that the Almighty bestowed on him.

8) Mention of their close relationships with famous scholars and preachers. Some people like to mention how much it is valued by any scholars or people known for their righteousness. Some students of Sharia may flaunt the fact that such and such a scholar had a personal conversation and in secret told him something that he did not tell anyone but him. Others will not fail to mention (even if no one asked them about it) that they took private lessons from such and such a sheikh, were visiting such and such, invited such and such to visit. This is also one of the types of self-deception and narcissism. Proximity to scholars and the righteous does not make a person a scholar or a righteous person. Remember the wife of the prophet Lut and the wife of the prophet Nuh, their closeness to the great prophets did nothing to help them, and they perished along with the dead. Good reviews of scholars and righteous people about someone are not a guarantee of spiritual purity of a person, because no one knows what the heart is fraught with. And if so, then what is the point of mentioning this, if not the desire to raise one's authority and get respect in the eyes of people? A Muslim should always watch his speech, and if he wants to say something, ask something or answer someone, then before starting to speak,

let him ask his soul what it wants to achieve
with the words that will now be said.

9) Belittling the opinions of other people in order to show oneself and assert one's own opinion. Such a person likes to fill his own worth by belittling others, he constantly urges with phrases like "do not fuss", "think before you do", "do not force things", "what would you do without me". Then he can give a whole list of teachings and recommendations in which he will present himself as a very wise and experienced person who knows life and understands what should be and how it should be.

Some scholars have said: "The tragedy of man is complacency. Whoever looks at his soul and considers it good will destroy it. Whoever does not find something to blame his soul for, he fell into self-deception."

Speaking of these pernicious qualities inherent in the human soul, we reveal the inner beauty and spiritual purity of truly believing people who were able to eradicate these pernicious qualities in themselves. How beautiful is that believer who does good deeds, but does not like anyone to mention them and attribute them to him. Who can be better than those who worship Allah, show sincerity and diligence in good deeds, but at the same time always feel their imperfection and humble themselves before the Almighty Lord?! What righteous deed can be more beautiful than that which is hidden from human eyes and which no one except Allah knows about?!

Addressing people who are engaged in the work of calling to Islam, ibn al-Jawzi said: "How few are those who do righteous deeds sincerely for the sake of Allah. Many people want their worship to be seen by others. If you stop caring about how people will evaluate you and stop gaining respect from them by doing righteous deeds, if you purify your intention and hide your pious deeds, then know that it is precisely such qualities that exalted great people."

Sheikh Sahl ibn Abdullah at-Tustari was asked: "What is the most difficult thing for the soul?" He replied: "Sincerity, because the soul has nothing of it." A sincere deed is done by a person not for the sake of his own benefits or any worldly interests, but for the sake of Allah.

Al-Hasan al-Basri (may Allah have mercy on him) once said: "It is reported that the one from whom Allah accepts one good deed from his deeds, He will admit him to Paradise." Then the disciples asked him: "O Abu Said, where will all the other good deeds of the servants of Allah go?!" Al-Hasan replied: "Verily, Allah (He is Great and Glorious) accepts only pure (sincere) and good deeds, in which there is no place for narcissism and show-off, and the one who has at least one good deed will correspond to this, will be among successful."

10) Mentioning your employment in order to fill your worth. When some people are asked for help, they immediately refuse and ask for forgiveness, and they have the right to do so. But sometimes, at the same time, a person begins to spread about how busy he is, that he has a lot of important things to do and obligations. Moreover, some believe that it is fashionable to pretend to be a busy and business person. In this regard, the words of one woman are recalled, whose husband told her that he was very busy with the affairs of Islam and the call, that he did not even have time to pay attention to her. To this the woman replied: "I think that this is either being astute or showing-off." Either he says something that is not true, or simply wants to raise his own worth in the eyes of his wife, and if not, is he really more busy with the affairs of Islam than the Messenger of Allah (peace and blessings of Allah be upon him) and righteous scholars?

Dear brothers and sisters, despite the fact that all these words were written in the third person, this does not mean that according to this list we should judge the people around us and classify them as sincere and insincere. We must address all these points only to ourselves and make sure that nothing of the kind exists in ourselves.

All the good deeds that we do are really small compared to the mercy of Allah shown to us, even if these deeds are like high mountains in our eyes. While doing good deeds, keep fear and hope in your heart. Ibn Auf said: "Don't be too sure of your many good deeds, for you don't know whether they are accepted or not. The future fate of your deeds is completely hidden from you."

Do not forget to protect your righteous deeds with sincerity and purity of intentions, doing them only for the sake of Allah. Hide your good deeds just as you hide your sins, and if you managed to keep your intentions pure and do it only for the sake of Allah, then rejoice and hope in His mercy (He is Great and Glorious). Ibn Taymiyyah (may Allah grant him mercy) said: "Even one kind of worship that a person performs with absolute sincerity and dedicates it only to Allah, can cause Allah to forgive him his great sins. However, this is the case only with those who say these words (testimonies of Islam) as sincerely and honestly as this person said them. After all, it is known that people who commit great sins will enter Hell, and at the same time they all speak the words of Monotheism". Also, commenting on the hadith about the prostitute who watered the dog, and Allah forgave her sins, Ibn Taymiyyah (Allah have mercy on him) said: "This woman watered the dog with pure, sincere Faith in her heart, and her sins were forgiven, because not every prostitute who waters the dog has her sins forgiven. Actions differ in the degree of their righteousness, just as the degrees of faith and being God-fearing differ in the hearts of people."

Dear brothers and sisters, remember that there are three diseases for showing off:

1) Love for praise and approval from people.

2) Fear of censure from people.

3) Passionate desire to get what others have: wealth, authority and other benefits.

These are dangerous diseases that can cause a bad end to life, because the one who is ill with these ailments lives in contradiction with himself, his inner world is opposite to the outer one. In this regard, it is appropriate to recall the words of al-Hasan al-Basri, who said: "May Allah bestow his mercy on a person who is not deceived by the many things that he sees in other people. O son of Adam! You will endure death alone, you will enter the grave alone, you will rise again alone, and you will receive your account alone."

We ask Allah to make all our deeds correct and pure before His Blessed Face. We ask Him to deliver us from showing off, narcissism, love of fame and other harmful properties of our souls. All mercy comes only from Allah, he led us on the straight path, gave us everything that we have, and taught us what we did not know.

Praise be to Allah, peace and blessings be upon our Prophet Muhammad, as well as his family and all his companions.

Dear Muslim brothers and Muslim sisters, fear your Lord and remember the words of Allah:

"Fear the day when you will be returned to Allah. Then each person will receive in full what he has acquired, and they will not be treated unfairly."
(Quran 2:281)

Islam is beliefs and actions, faith in Allah and Monotheism, faith in angels and holy books, faith in messengers and Judgment Day, faith in the predestination of everything, both good and bad. Islam is pure worship of Allah alone, complete humility before Him, absolute contentment with His Religion, and faith in the Messenger of Allah (peace and blessings of Allah be upon him) without the slightest doubt, hesitation and embarrassment.

Islam is following the path of the prophet (peace and blessings of Allah be upon him) in deeds, in relationships with people and in their judgments, in their decisions and ways of implementing them, both for individuals and for entire societies.

Islam is a life of worship. The main goal and main aspiration of the heart of a Muslim is his

Lord and the desire to please Him with all his deeds.

Oh slaves of Allah! Purification of one's religion before Allah is the basis of religion, it is the essence of Monotheism and worship. With his good deeds, a person should strive only for the Face of Allah, His reward and mercy. He is obliged to confess the six pillars of the Faith (*Iman*), to fulfill the five pillars of Islam, to bring his Faith to perfection (*Ihsan*), to observe the rights of Allah and the rights of people, striving only for the Face of the Almighty and the Eternal Abode, not wanting to achieve the approval of people, fame, power or any of the blessings of this world. This is perfect Faith and perfect Monotheism.

Most of all, this contradicts when a person does righteous deeds for the sake of people's praise and their respect, or when he does good deeds in order to receive transient worldly goods, this destroys the purity of the Faith and Monotheism. Allah (Holy and Great is He) said in the Noble Quran, in Surah Hud:

"To those who desire the life of the world and its adornments, We will fully repay their deeds

in this world, and they will therein not be deprived."
(Quran 11:15)

The Almighty explained to us in this verse that the performance of righteous deeds for the sake of the benefits of this perishable life violates the degree of completeness of Monotheism, which is necessary for a person to be considered a true monotheist, and destroys these righteous deeds. This is even worse than showing (*riya*), because if a person desires this world with his heart, then, as a rule, this desire absorbs all his deeds, and showing off can manifest itself only in individual actions and does not always accompany a person in all his actions.

There is a difference between showing off and wanting this world by doing righteous deeds:

The show-off and the one who wants to achieve the blessings of this world with righteous deeds are united in that each of them, doing good deeds, does not strive to get closer to Allah and deserve eternal life in Paradise, both of them commit a small *shirk* (*shirk asghar*), which violates the necessary fullness and perfection of Monotheism.

The difference lies in the following:

The ostentatious person, through his righteous deeds, wants to get the approval of people and their positive feedback in his address, his showing off can manifest itself in certain actions, but not in all deeds.

The one who wants to achieve worldly goods with his righteous deeds, he is looking for material gain, such as money, power, position in society, and such a desire prevails in most of his good deeds.

Ad-Dahhak (may Allah grant him mercy) said: "The one from the people of the Faith who does any righteous deed without piety (*taqwa*) will receive a quick reward for his deed in this world" (i.e. a person can receive reward in this world, and then he will completely lose it in the World to Come).

Abu Qatada (may Allah have mercy on him) said: "The Almighty informed us that if the greatest concern, desire and aspiration of a person is this world, then Allah will reward him in this world. Then he will go to the World to Come and he will not find any good deeds for which he could receive a reward. As for the believer, he receives a reward for his good deeds, both in this world and in the Next."

In an authentic hadith narrated by Abu Hurayrah, it is said that the Messenger of Allah (peace and blessings of Allah be upon him) said:

"The first people to be judged will be those who memorized the Quran completely, those who were killed in the way of Allah and those who had a lot of wealth. And then Allah will say to the reciter [of the Quran]:

"Have I not taught you what was sent down to My Messenger?"

The recitor will answer:

"Yes, oh Lord."

Allah will say:

What did you do with your knowledge?

The reader will answer:

"I stood [reading the Quran in my prayers] day and night."

And Allah will say:

- You are lying.

And the angels will say:

- You are lying.

And Allah will say to him:

You just wanted to be called "such and such a reader of the Quran" and they said so.

Then this hadith mentions the owner of wealth, who spent his money on charity and a fighter who fell in the battle for the religion of Allah, and they have a similar dialogue with the Almighty Lord, and at the end, Allah says to the rich man: You only wanted people to say "such and such generous man", and Allah says to the insincere *Mujahid*: You only wanted people to say "such and such a brave man" and people really said so.

At the end of the hadith, the Messenger of Allah (peace and blessings of Allah be upon him) said: "Oh, Abu Hurairah, these will be the first people who will kindle the Fire on the Day of Judgment, these people had some deeds, but they did not want the Face of Allah with these deeds." When Abu Hurairah was asked about this hadeeth, he almost fainted. It is also known that Muawiyah (may Allah be pleased with him) also almost fainted when he heard this hadeeth and said: Allah said the truth:

"To those who desire the life of the near world and its adornments, We will fully repay their deeds in this world, and they will not be deprived therein."
(Quran 11:15)

Speaking about this verse, the righteous predecessors (salafu salih) mentioned several types of deeds that are committed by people today, but people sometimes do not understand that their actions are also condemned by this verse.

First view. Sometimes people do some righteous deed, dedicating it only to Allah, perform prayers, give alms, connect family ties, help people, move away from crimes and sins and do other good deeds that should be done for the sake of Allah, but at the same time they do not want rewards for them in the Next Life. They do this so that Allah rewards them in this life, preserves and increases their property, protects their families and relatives, does not deprive them of their well-being and does not cease to bestow them with blessings. These people don't care much about entering Paradise and avoiding Hell. Such people will be given their reward in this life, and in the Next Life they will receive nothing for their deeds. Ibn Abbas (may Allah be pleased with him) mentioned this type of people.

Second kind. This view is worse and more terrible than the first. The Mujahid said that this verse was sent down precisely in relation to this group of people... These are those who do righteous deeds with the intention of appearing before people, and not in order to achieve a reward in the World to Come.

Third kind. These are people who perform righteous deeds with the intention of getting money for it, for example: performing the hajj for a reward in order to earn money, performing the *hijra* in order to obtain worldly goods, participating in a holy war in order to receive a share in trophies, gaining knowledge in order to gain honor and leadership over people, studying the Quran and diligently attending the mosque in order to get some position in the mosque, etc. This type of people were mentioned in some *tafseers* of this verse.

Fourth kind . This type includes those who do deeds of worship to Allah sincerely, but at the same time they do deeds of disbelief, which deprives them of Faith and leads them out of Islam. These include Jews, Christians and some people who identify themselves as Muslims. They submit to Allah, perform rites of worship with absolute sincerity, desire to achieve the reward of the Almighty, but at the same time they do deeds that remove them from Islam and this prevents them from accepting their good deeds. This type of people were mentioned by Anas ibn Malik and other scholars when interpreting the above verse. The righteous predecessors were afraid to be among these people, some of them said: "If I knew that Allah accepted at least one earthly bow (sujud) from me, I would wish to die on this, because Allah Almighty said:

"Indeed, Allah only accepts from the pious."
(Quran 5:27)

In an authentic hadith from the words of Abu Hurayrah, it is reported that the Messenger of

Allah (peace and blessings of Allah be upon him) said:

"May the slave of the dinar perish, may the slave of the dirham perish, may the slave of silk and velvet robes perish, who shows satisfaction when he is given something and gets angry when he is not given. May he perish and be turned over, and even if a thorn pricks him, may he not extract it."

The Messenger of Allah (peace and blessings of Allah be upon him) offered a prayer so that the worshipers of this world would perish and be unhappy, and that any business in this life would be difficult for them, and that they could not solve their most insignificant problems and could not even get rid of from the thorn that pricked them.

The Prophet (peace and blessings of Allaah be upon him) called them slaves of dinars and dirhams for their unbridled passion for hoarding, and for the fact that they perform deeds of worship in order to earn these dinars and dirhams. Such feelings as contentment and anger, he shows only for the sake of material wealth, he does not show contentment for the sake of Allah and does not get angry for the sake of Allah. In this position, a person falls into a small polytheism (*shirk asgar*), which violates the perfection and purity of Monotheism.

This is the destiny of those who have tied their hearts to this world, to power, wealth and other base desires of the soul. When they are given something to which their hearts are attached, they rejoice; when they are deprived of it, they feel resentment and anger. These are true slaves and worshipers of their desires, because true slavery and worship is in the heart. What the heart is captivated in this world, the owner of this heart will serve. In this position is also the one who unrestrainedly pursues wealth, it enslaves him, makes him unquestioningly obey himself. The attachment of the heart to worldly goods is of two types:

1) A person's heartfelt attachment to those things that he needs, such as: food, drink, marriage, housing, vehicle, home decoration. A person who suffers from a strong attachment to these goods is fearful, anxious, not steadfast in his Religion.

2) Heart attachment to things that he does not need, to things for which a person should not have any attachment at all. If a person is

attached to what he does not need, then he becomes a slave of these things, and ceases to be a true slave of Allah and to rely on Him, and the root of polytheism grows in his heart.

The Messenger of Allah (peace and blessings of Allah be upon him) said:

"May Paradise (Tuba) be granted to that person who holds his horse by the bridle in the path of Allah, with disheveled hair, with feet covered with dust, if he is put on guard, then he stands guard, if left in the rear, then he carries service in the rear, if he asks for permission, he is not given permission, if he intercedes for someone, then his intercession is not accepted."

The Messenger of Allah (peace and blessings of Allah be upon him) explained to us that in Paradise there is a reward for those who, with their righteous deeds, sought only the Face of Allah and His contentment, despite the fact that he himself is in a difficult life situation. The Prophet (peace and blessings of Allah be upon him) praised the sincere fighter for the Faith in this hadith and characterized him with five qualities:

1) "holds his horse by the bridle", that is, he does not part with his horse on the path of Allah, constantly striving to fight for the triumph of Islam.

2) "with disheveled hair", - the struggle in the path of Allah distracted him from comfortable conditions and a pleasant life.

3) "with feet covered with dust" - he does not sit still, he is always busy with long transitions and is ready to rush into battle.

4) "if he is put on guard, then he is on guard, if he is left in the rear, then he is serving in the rear," - if he is left on guard or on patrol, then he responsibly and efficiently performs the duty assigned to him. And he forces himself to perform tasks that are not the most pleasant for him for the sake of jihad, wanting to receive a reward from Allah (He is Great and Glorious). Ibn Jawzi (may Allah grant him mercy) said: "This is an obscure warrior, he does not strive for greatness, where it fell to him to serve there he is serving, guards and service in the rear guard of the troops were mentioned in the hadith, because in reality it is harder".

5) "if he asks for permission, he is not given permission, if he intercedes for someone, then his intercession is not accepted" - if, of necessity, he turns to the command with some kind of request, or intercedes for someone in a charitable cause , then he does not receive permission, and his petition is not accepted, since this warrior is not noble and does not have a high position. This warrior is not busy seeking high positions and ranks, he is busy seeking the contentment and reward of Allah, and does not expect a return from his righteous deeds in this life.

It is not at all because Allah neglects his sincere believer a slave, but on the contrary, it is mercy for him. This hadeeth clearly indicates that an insignificant position in front of people does not mean an insignificant position in front of Allah (He is Great and Glorious). The hadeeth says that a sincere Muslim who does his work for the sake of Allah does not care what work he has been assigned to do if this work is pleasing to God. If he was appointed a responsible person or commander, then he performs his duties in the best way, but if he was entrusted with less authoritative work, then he accepts this with satisfaction, and tries to do it in the best way. A sincere Muslim seeks to benefit his Ummah, wherever he is and whatever he does.

"We will take care of their deeds that they have committed and turn them into scattered dust."
(Quran 25:23)

The cases of infidels such as Jews, Christians and representatives of other religions will not be accepted. If they fed and helped the poor, treated the sick and did other good deeds, then all this is destroyed by their unbelief in Allah Almighty. But still, the justice of Allah gives them the opportunity to receive the reward, which is mentioned in the following hadith. The Messenger of Allah (peace and blessings of Allah be upon him) said:

"If an unbeliever does any good deed, then he will be granted some portion of this world for this" (Muslim narrated the hadith).

Allah Almighty said:

"Those who desire life in this world and its adornments, We will fully repay their deeds in this world, and they will not be deprived."
(Quran 11:15)

If a person does righteous deeds, desiring only the blessings of this world, then his deed is not valid, and it is completely rejected by Allah. If a person desires the blessings of this world and the World to Come, then his work is flawed, due to the loss of the integrity of sincere intentions. A sincere believer does good deeds, striving only for the Face of Allah and the eternal Paradise Abode. If a believer seeks knowledge, he does so in order to eradicate his ignorance and benefit people. If he makes a Hajj (pilgrimage) to the House of Allah for a deceased or elderly incapable person, then he does this with the aim of helping his brother in the Faith, visiting holy places and walking this path along with other pilgrims. If he gives alms to the poor, he does it in order to instill joy in their hearts and save them from sorrow and suffering. If he fights he does it only to raise the banner of Islam. Indeed, Allah our Lord is Generous, He rewards the believer for his good deeds, both in this world and in the World to Come. Allah (He is Great and Glorious) protects him, his family and property, makes his life blessed and calm, and in the Next Life he will be rewarded in the best way.

If a person sincerely and for the sake of Allah performs any charitable deed in which there is a public benefit for Muslims, then they can provide for his needs by paying him a certain amount. This is done in order to free this person from the need to spend time earning money and do only what is necessary for Muslims. These cases include such activities as: the work of a *Sharia* judge, holding five times collective prayers in a mosque, teaching people the Quran. Receiving this money will not harm the Faith and Monotheism of a Muslim, if he regards them only as helping him to perform good socially useful deeds. The Messenger of Allah (peace and blessings of Allah be upon him) said:

"The Book of Allah is most worthy of you taking payment for it" (narrated by al-Bukhari).

Allah Almighty said: "Say (Muhammad): I am only a man like you: a revelation was sent down to me that your God is One God. And whoever hopes to meet his Lord, let him do a good deed and, in worshiping his Lord, associate no one with Him"
(Surah Kahf, 110) .

Allah Almighty also said: "... and they were ordered only to worship Allah, keeping sincerity to Him in religion ..." (Surah al-Baiyinah, 5) .

Indeed, sincerity towards Allah is the true essence of religion and the key to understanding why the Messengers of Allah, peace be upon them, turned to people with their call.

Allah Almighty said:
"And who professes religion better than the one who obeys Allah and does good deeds ...?"
(Surah Nisa, 125).

Allah Almighty and Great also said: "... who created death and life to test you: which of you is best in deed." (Surah al-Mulk, 2).

Regarding this, al-Fudayl gave the following explanation:
"This means: who will be the most sincere and most correct?"

It is reported that Abu Hurayrah, may Allah be pleased with him, said that he heard the Messenger of Allah (peace and blessings of Allah be upon him) say, that Allah said: "They gave me partners, and if someone does something not only for my sake, then I will leave him and his polytheism". (Muslim)

Ibn Rajab said: "Know that deeds not done for the sake of Allah are of several types. Sometimes this is outright show-off, as is the case with the hypocrites about whom the Almighty said:
"And when they get up for Salah (prayer), they get up lazy, pretending before people and only occasionally remembering Allah." (Surah Nisa, 142).

Such frank show-off is almost never found among believers during obligatory Salah and fasting, however, it can appear when giving alms, performing an obligatory great pilgrimage and other worship.

Abu Sa'id narrated the following saying of the Prophet:

"Shall I tell you what is more dangerous and terrible for you than al-Masih ad-Dajjal?"

The people said: "Yes, O Messenger of Allah!"

He said: "It is hidden polytheism: when a person stands up for Salah, specially exaggerating it, when he sees that someone is looking at him". (Ahmad, Ibn Maja)

Here it should be recalled that if people show sincerity in the performance of certain religious duties, doing it only for the sake of Allah, then we see that Allah makes the reward of such sincere people great, and their reward is great even in cases where the person appear to be doing little or a minor action of worship. About this, Ibn Taymiyyah says this: "The only type of deeds for which Allah forgives great sins, as indicated in one of the hadiths are such deeds, by which a person shows absolute sincerity and serves only Allah."

Abdullah ibn Amr ibn al-As narrated a hadeeth which states:"On the Day of Resurrection, one person from my community will be called before all creatures, and ninety-nine books of sins will be unfolded before him, each of which does not encompass the gaze. Then he will be asked: "Do you deny any of this?" He will answer: "No, O Lord!" He will be asked: "Do you have an excuse or a good deed?" This person will be confused with fright and will say: "No." Then they will say to him: "Yes! We have one good deed of yours, and you will not be treated unfairly today." Then they will bring a piece of paper in front of him with the words "I testify that there is no deity but Allah and that Muhammad is His servant and messenger." Then he will say: "O Lord! What is the weight of this sheet compared to these books?" They will say to him: "Today you will not be treated unfairly." Then they will put the books on one side of the balance, and the leaf on the other, and the books will be light, and the leaf will be heavy. (at-Tirmidhi, Ahmad and others)

Thus, a person who pronounces evidence of monotheism must be sincere and truthful, since sincerity was shown by the one referred to in the aforementioned hadith, otherwise these words lose all meaning, because the same evidence was uttered by all the rest of those who committed grave sins, and ended up in hell, but unlike that man, their testimonies did not outweigh their bad deeds.

Then Ibn Taymiyyah cites another hadith, which speaks of a prostitute who gave water to a thirsty dog, for which Allah forgave her her sins, and another hadith, which reports that Allah forgave a person who removed from the path that which prevented others from walking, after which he writes:

- This woman gave water to the dog, keeping pure faith in her heart, for which she received forgiveness, and if this were not so, then every prostitute who gave water to the dog would be forgiven ... Thus, the superiority of some deeds over others is determined by the degree of faith kept by hearts, and the degree of their reverence for Allah.

On the other hand, we find that the performance of any religious duty, devoid of sincerity and truthfulness, has no value and is not rewarded in any way. Moreover, people who perform their religious duties in this way are subject to the threats of Allah, even if they do something very important, such as spending their funds or donating their wealth to charity, participating in battles against the infidels, or gaining knowledge of Sharia.

# DEFINITION OF SINCERNITY AND ITS LIMITS

With regard to the definition and boundaries of sincerity, the ulema spoke on this subject in different ways.

Some define sincerity as the desire to fulfill one's religious duties only for the sake of Allah Almighty.

Others say: "Sincerity is the liberation of action from the supervision of people."

Abu Ali al-Fadil ibn Iyad said: "Deeds are not accepted if they were sincere, but were not correct, or were correct, but were not sincere, until they become sincere and correct. What is done for the sake of Allah, and what is right is that which is in accordance with the Sunnah."

Al-Kharawi said: "Sincerity is the liberation of deeds from any foreign impurities."

One of them said: "A sincere person is one who does not attach any importance to the fact that he means nothing to the hearts of others, for his own heart has become righteous before Allah Almighty, and therefore he does not want people to know even about the most insignificant of his affairs."

There is no doubt that great effort must be made to achieve complete sincerity.

It is reported that once Sahl bin Abdullah at-Tustari was asked: "What is the most difficult for the soul?" He replied: "Sincerity, because there is no inheritance for the soul in it."

Sufyan as-Thawri said: "I have never dealt with anything more difficult for me than my intentions, for they are changeable."

ABOUT SUBTLE MANIFESTATIONS AND HIDDEN SIDES OF STRIVING FOR SHOWING OFF

Know that among the things that are incompatible with sincerity are love for this world, glory and honor, the desire for ostentation and narcissism.

In this particular case, the desire for ostentatious means worshiping Allah only for the sake of people seeing it and for them to give praise to the worshiper. This means that such a person seeks exaltation or glorification from other people, or wants to inspire those who see him with any desire or cause fear in them.

With regard to the desire for fame, it is implied to do the aforementioned deeds just for the sake of people hearing about them.

As for narcissism, it is inextricably linked with the desire to perform certain deeds for show, and the difference between the one and the other, Sheikh-ul-Islam Ibn Taymiyyah defines as follows:

"Doing something for show is related to such a manifestation of polytheism, when this is done not only for the sake of Allah, but also for the sake of people, and narcissism leads to such a manifestation of it, when something is done not only for the sake of Allah, but also for the sake of oneself "Al-Fataawa, 10/277.

And now, we will give some examples of subtle manifestations and hidden sides of the desire for ostentation. We are talking about only a few examples, since it is possible to talk about what is incompatible with sincerity for a very long time, while here it will be enough to point out only three subtle manifestations of the desire for ostentation, namely:

FIRST, this is what was mentioned by Abu Hamid al-Ghazali, who said the following about the secret desire for ostentation:
I would not consider the manifestations of inattention to myself on the part of people as something incredible. And although in everything that has to do with people, doing deeds of worship is not equivalent to not doing them, nevertheless he is not satisfied with the fact that Allah already knows about this, which means that such a person is not free from hidden and very subtle impurities of aspiration to show. All this can easily lead to the fact that such a person will lose his reward, and only the most truthful are free from this. "Ihya", 3/305-306.

SECONDLY, an example of this is the case when a person considers sincerity towards Allah not as an end in itself, but only as a means to achieve certain worldly goals.

Sheikh-ul-Islam, who warned about this secret disaster, said in particular: "It is said that someone said to Abu Hamid al-Ghazali that if a person maintains sincerity towards Allah for forty days, then the springs of wisdom, beating in his heart, they will beat on his tongue. Abu

Hamid said: "And I tried to do this for forty days, but it did not lead to anything. Then I told about this to one of the knowers (of the truth), who said to me: Verily, you showed sincerity only for the sake of wisdom, but not for the sake of Allah!"

Ibn Taymiyyah then writes: "The reason for this is that a person's goal may be to acquire knowledge and wisdom, or to achieve an ecstatic state, or to earn the respect of people and hear their praises, or anything else that can be achieved by showing sincerity towards Allah, however, the desire to achieve this through such a means as showing sincerity towards Allah is completely incompatible with this means, because if someone strives for something for the sake of something else, then the second is the desired goal, the first becomes only means of achieving it.Thus, if a person seeks to be sincere with Allah for the sake of knowledge, wisdom, achieving ecstasy or gaining control over something, this means that he does not strive for Allah, but makes Allah a means to some lower end..." Ad-Dar'u, 6/66-67.

And therefore, al-Shatibi (may Allah have mercy on him) says:

"If a capable person obeys a command or prohibition in this or that matter, not paying attention to anything other than this command or prohibition itself, this will mean that he renounced his own of his lot, began to fulfill his duties towards his Lord and began to behave like a slave. It will be different if he begins to pay attention to the consequences and take them into account, since in this case his desire will be directed towards the final result." In other words, his turning to his Lord will be due to the cause, since it will be mediated by his turning to the result. There is no doubt that there is a great difference between these two degrees of sincerity." Al-Muawafaqat, 1/219-220

And, THIRDLY, the subtle manifestations of the desire for show are related to what Ibn Rajab points out, may Allah have mercy on him, who said: "But there is one subtle point, the essence of which is that a person can begin to blame himself in the presence of others, trying to make people think that he is inwardly maintaining humility, as a result of which he will be exalted in their eyes, and they will begin to praise him. This indicates the presence of subtle manifestations of the desire for ostentation, to which our righteous predecessors paid attention. So, Mutrif bin Abdullah al-Shihkhir said: "To exalt the soul, it is enough for you to start blaming it, in fact, wanting to aggrandize it, which is shamelessness before Allah."

## TREATMENT OF THE DESIRE FOR SHOW-OFF

For every disease there is a cure, which some know about and others do not. There are various cures for such diseases as the desire for show and everything that is incompatible with sincerity, and among other things, these include the following:

1) - Every able-bodied Muslim should well understand that he is none other than the slave of Allah, and the slave has no right to compensation or payment for the service of his Master, since he must serve him by virtue of His position. As for the payment or reward that he can receive, this is not a recompense, but a manifestation of mercy and good deed on the part of his master.

2) - Understanding that Allah gives him mercy and assistance, that he is able to do something not by himself, but only with the help of Allah,

and that his actions are due to the will of Allah, and not his own desires ... Thus, any goodness is nothing but the mercy of Allah Almighty.

3) - The study of one's own shortcomings and omissions and the desire to understand what comes from the person himself and what comes from the shaitan, since there are few such cases in which the shaitan would not have had a hand, even if his role would be insignificant.

It is reported that Aisha, may Allah be pleased with her, said:
"(Once) I asked the Messenger of Allah (peace and blessings of Allah be upon him) about the turning of a person in different directions during prayer, he replied: "This is what the shaitan steals from the prayer of a servant."

But if here we are talking about turning the body, then what can be said about turning the heart to something other than Allah?!

4) - A reminder to the soul that Allah ordered to strive for perfection and purification of the heart, and also that a person who does something for show to others will be deprived of the help and assistance of Allah.

5) - The fear that when Allah sees the desire of the heart for show, this will cause His hatred.

6) - Trying to do things of worship in secret as much as possible, for example, praying at night, giving alms without anyone knowing about it, crying for fear of Allah alone when no one sees you.

Al-Khuraibi said: "They considered it desirable that a person do good deeds so secretly that neither his wife nor other people knew about it."

7) - A manifestation of respect for Allah Almighty, expressed in the confession of monotheism and worship of Allah and extending to His most beautiful names and highest attributes.

8) - A constant memory of death with its agony, the grave with its horrors and the Last Day, the events of which will make even babies turn gray.

9) - The effort to know the hidden sides of the desire for ostentation and how this desire is formed in the human soul in order to be able to protect oneself from such things.

10) - Understanding what consequences in this world and in the world to come can entail the performance of actions for show to others.

The servant of Allah must understand that even if all people gather in order to do something useful for him, they will only be able to do what Allah has already predetermined for him, as the Prophet (peace and blessings of Allaah be upon him) spoke about in his instruction Ibn Abbas, may Allah be pleased with them both. And that is why one of our predecessors said: "He who knows (the limits of) people will find peace."

Another said this: "Fight with your soul to remove from yourself everything that pushes you to showiness, strive to ensure that people become like animals or small children for you, for when you are engaged in deeds of worship, it makes no difference to you whether they are present, or whether animals and children know about it or not, whether they know it or remain ignorant, and be content that only Allah will know about it."

And may Allah be pleased with Umar, who said:
"Allah will protect from people the one whose intentions will be connected only with the truth,

even contrary to the desires of his soul, and defame the one who will seek to adorn himself with something that is not really in him."

Ibn al-Qayyim said:

"Since a person who seeks to adorn himself with what is not his own is the opposite of the sincere and tries to show people something opposite to what he really is, Allah responds to him by leading him to what is opposite to his goal, and the like punishment is established by Shari'ah and predetermined, and when a sincere slave for his sincerity receives a reward in this world in the form of sympathy, love and respect in the hearts of people, the same applies to the one who seeks to adorn himself with what he does not actually possess, and therefore soon the punishment for him is that Allah covers him with disgrace among people, since he himself has disgraced himself before Allah, and this is in full accordance with the most beautiful names of the Lord and His highest attributes".

As for the punishment for ostentatious deeds that the guilty person will suffer in this eternal world, the Prophet (peace and blessings of Allaah be upon him) said about this: "Allah will glorify the one who tries to be heard by others, and expose the one who will do something for show to others." Al-Bukhari and Muslim.

In addition, from the hadith narrated by Abu Hurairah, may Allah be pleased with him, which was quoted above, it follows that people who do something good for show to others will be the first to be in the flames of hell.

11) - It is necessary to turn to Allah with prayers so that He will help you to be sincere and protect you from striving for show. This means that a Muslim should turn to Allah more often with requests that He protect him from striving for ostentatiousness and everything that induces a person to this, the need for which is indicated by a hadith in which it is reported that the Messenger of Allah (peace be upon him Allah (peace and blessings be upon him) said:

"The polytheism (hidden) in you is more inconspicuous than a crawling ant, but I will show you that thanks to which you will be able to get rid of both small and large (manifestations) of polytheism. Say: O Allah, indeed I seek Your protection from worshiping anyone else besides You knowingly, and ask You for forgiveness for what I myself do not know..." (Sahih al-Jami' as-saghir", 3/233).

And in conclusion, we ask Allah to save us from showing off and grant us sincerity!

www.ingramcontent.com/pod-product-compliance
Lightning Source LLC
Chambersburg PA
CBHW021321160726
47994CB00004B/1557